D0382578

Saving Manatees

Saving Manatees

Stephen R. Swinburne

BOYDS MILLS PRESS

Honesdale, Pennsylvania

3120200036861W

ACKNOWLEDGMENTS

Many thanks to John E. Reynolds III, Ph.D., manatee research program manager at Mote Marine Laboratory, Sarasota, Florida; Andy Garrett and Alex Costidis, marine biologists, Florida Fish and Wildlife Marine Mammal Pathology Laboratory; Bonnie Abellera, Florida Fish and Wildlife Conservation Commission; Dr. Mark Lowe, Midway Veterinary Clinic; and Nancy Sadusky, Save the Manatee Club.

—S. R. S.

Text and photographs copyright © 2006 by Stephen R. Swinburne
Additional photographs and images courtesy of:
Florida Fish & Wildlife Conservation Commission: pp. title page, 7, 11, 18, 19 (left), 20, 21, 27(right), 36
Pieter Folkens: p. 15
Sammie Garnett, pp. 10 (left), 16 (left), 17, 22, 26 (top), 28, 31, 34
Joe Bauer Griffin, p. 40
Mark Lowe, Midway Veterinary Clinic: p. 19 (right)
John Reynolds, Mote Marine Lab: p. 14 (right)
Patrick Rose, Save the Manatee Club: pp. 8 (left), 33 (left)
Tampa's Lowry Park Zoo, pp. 26 (bottom), 27 (left), 29, 39

Boyds Mills Press, Inc.
A Highlights Company
815 Church Street
Honesdale, Pennsylvania 18431
Printed in China

Library of Congress Cataloging-in-Publication Data

Swinburne, Stephen R.
  Saving manatees / by Stephen Swinburne.—1st ed.
     p. cm.
  Includes bibliographical references.
  ISBN-13: 978-1-59078-319-1 (hardcover : alk. paper)
  1. Manatees—Florida—Juvenile literature. I. Title.

  QL737.S63S95 2006
  599.5509759—dc22

                                        2006000523

First edition, 2006
The text of this book is set in 13-point Minion.

Visit our Web site at www.boydsmillspress.com

10 9 8 7 6 5 4 3 2 1

To my Florida friend and an awesome educator, Sammie Garnett. I'd search for manatees with you anytime. And to the young manatee that I had a close encounter with at Crystal River National Wildlife Refuge—may your kind live peacefully forever

—S. R. S.

A manatee grazes on hydrilla, one of the manatee's favorite foods.

(left) *A bulbous-faced, piggy-eyed, torpedo-shaped manatee paddles Florida waters. Aerial surveys put the state's manatee population at around 3,000 animals. Florida began recording manatee populations in 1974. In 2005, 396 manatees died from a variety of causes, including 80 from boat collisions and 81 from red tide. In 1973, Congress passed the Endangered Species Act, classifying manatees as endangered. Over thirty years later, there is a movement underway in Florida to change the status of manatees from endangered to threatened. This could lift restrictions on boat speeds and waterfront development.*

Chapter One

MANATEE HEAVEN

I DARE YOU TO LOOK INTO THE FACE OF A MANATEE and not fall in love. A manatee is like nothing you've ever seen. You may see it as a hodgepodge of animals, but a manatee is a unique creature. Close up, manatees have the whiskers of a walrus, the eyes of a mole, the wrinkles and toenails of an elephant, the tail of a beaver, and the gentle nature of a sloth. Manatees are slow-moving, water-loving, plant-eating, gentle gray giants.

On a brisk April morning, I shove my hand and a thermometer into the chilly waters of the West River, beside my house in southern Vermont. The thermometer reads forty-three degrees Fahrenheit. A few months earlier, I stood in a warm-water spring in Florida. The water temperature was seventy-four degrees. Manatees in a rehabilitation enclosure surrounded me. They wouldn't last long in my Vermont river. Manatees need warm water. In water below sixty to sixty-five degrees Fahrenheit, manatees may get cold stress. Inside they

A calf nurses from a mother manatee.

MANATEE FACTS
MOTHER MANATEE

Manatees begin breeding when they're about five years old. They are slow breeders. Females produce one calf every three to five years. Manatees can live as long as fifty to sixty years but often do not live that long in the wild. If a female manatee gives birth about every five years starting at age five, a manatee might have two to three calves in a lifetime. Calves remain with their mothers for up to two years. The young manatees nurse from mammary glands located at the "armpit" (between the flipper and body) of the mother. Within a few weeks of birth, young manatees begin eating plants. The male doesn't help raise the young.

may be as hot as a furnace and they may have skin and blubber the thickness of a filet mignon, yet manatees stay where the water is warm.

The type of manatee found in Florida lives in the southeastern United States, in the Caribbean Sea, and as far south as the Brazilian coast. There are just over three thousand manatees living in Florida's salt, brackish, or fresh water. About half of Florida's manatees live on the Atlantic coast and the other half on the Gulf coast. In summer, when the water temperature rises, manatees wander north to the shores of Georgia and the Carolinas, as well as to the coasts of Alabama, Mississippi, Louisiana, and Texas. Once, a manatee swam all the way from Florida to Rhode Island and back.

I must be in manatee heaven. I'm standing on an elevated boardwalk on the edge of a wide freshwater river. On the opposite bank, an alligator, all twelve feet of resting reptile,

Manatees use their flippers to steer, to crawl along the river bottom, and to put food into their mouths.

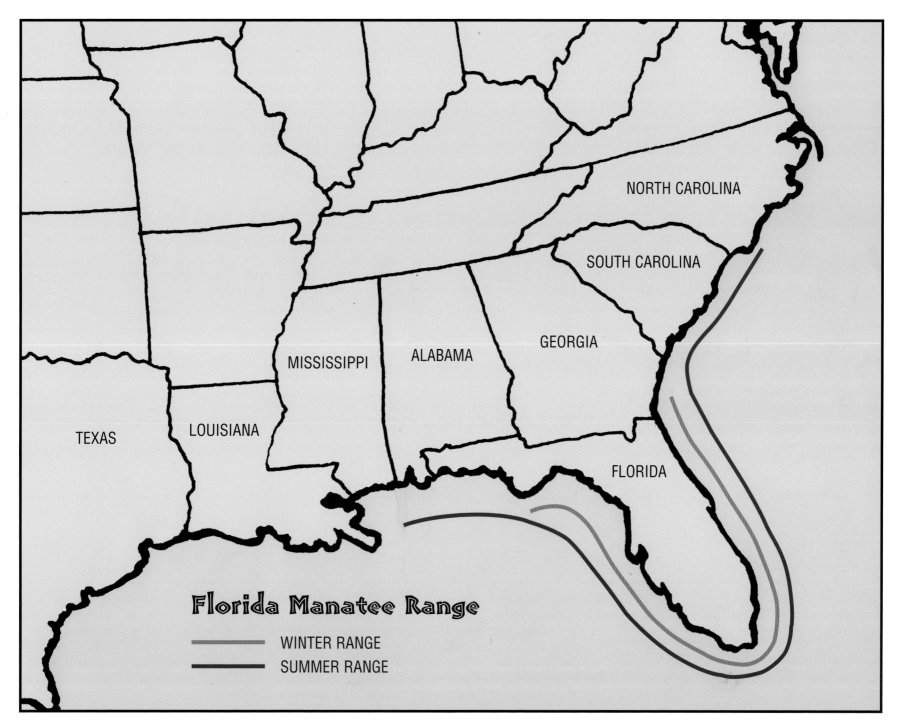

NORTH CAROLINA

SOUTH CAROLINA

GEORGIA

MISSISSIPPI   ALABAMA

FLORIDA

TEXAS   LOUISIANA

Florida Manatee Range

WINTER RANGE
SUMMER RANGE

I scan the waters of Blue Spring State Park for manatees.

*Manatees squeak and chirp, which is how mother and calf
stay in touch.*

basks in sultry Florida sunshine. Live oak trees with broad branches festooned with waving gray beards of Spanish moss hang over the still water. In the cloudless blue sky, bald eagles and ospreys dip and wheel. Through crystal-clear water—eight feet deep—mullet, catfish, garr, and bass swim. Two manatees, like slow-motion torpedoes, glide in from a weed-choked part of the river. They barrel-roll directly in front of me. I feel as if I'm in a nature movie.

I think that if I were a manatee I'd want to hang out at Blue Spring State Park. The park is an hour north of Orlando, Florida. Perhaps it's this lazy afternoon day, but time seems

to stand still here. And maybe that's not such a bad thing for a manatee.

Because manatees may be running out of time.

A relative of the manatee, called the Steller's sea cow, lived along islands in the Arctic waters of the Bering Strait. Steller's sea cows were three times longer than manatees. In 1741, a party of Russian explorers shipwrecked on the barren shores. The survivors discovered sea cows and learned that they moved slowly and could be hunted easily. Over the next twenty-seven years, people killed them for their meat and blubber. By 1768, the Steller's sea cow was extinct. It took people a short twenty-seven years to wipe out an entire species.

Can we learn something from past generations? Will you be able to tell your children or your grandchildren that in the clear waters of Florida swims a gentle mammal called a manatee?

MANATEE FACTS
MANATEES ARE BIG EATERS

Manatees and dugongs are the only two marine mammals that are herbivores, or vegetarians. Manatees spend a lot of time eating, about six to eight hours a day. They can consume more than one hundred pounds of water plants in twenty-four hours. Imagine eating more than two hundred heads of lettuce! Manatees enjoy a wide variety of green stuff. In salt water, manatees eat turtle grass, manatee grass, and shoal grass. Along the coasts, they consume mangrove leaves and seedlings. They eat lots of freshwater plants, including water hyacinth, water lettuce, eelgrass, and hydrilla.

Manatees will partially haul themselves out of the water to eat grass. A biologist once said, "If it's green and not moving fast, a manatee will eat it."

Both state and federal laws protect manatees. If you are operating a boat and see the above sign, slow down.

(left) The natural warm-water springs found in the headwaters of the Homosassa River in northwestern Florida are an important wintering area for manatees.

Chapter Two

Manatees Get a Checkup

I LOOK LIKE A FISH OUT OF WATER in a bad-fitting walrus costume. I'm wearing a black wet suit and standing in knee-deep water at a place called Homosassa Springs Wildlife State Park, Florida. The part of me underwater is toasty warm. The water temperature is seventy-four degrees Farenheit. The part of me above water is freezing. The air temperature is thirty-five degrees, with a north wind blowing. This is my first time in a wet suit in more than twenty years. It doesn't fit right. It feels clammy. I feel like an idiot.

And then I see the manatee. All thoughts of my discomfort pass. The first thing that strikes me about manatees is their size. They seem as big as a Volkswagen Bug, as wide as a rowboat, as long as a lunch table. But for all their size, they move

A manatee's skin is finely wrinkled with sparse hairs growing over the entire body. The skin continually sloughs off, or sheds, which reduces the buildup of algae and other aquatic growth.

as smoothly and gracefully as mermaids. I'm not sure I can agree with early sailors like Christopher Columbus, who in 1493 first saw the manatee from a distance and described it as a mermaid. According to the log of his famous voyage to the New World, Columbus recorded in his journal that he and his crew had seen three mermaids rise high from the sea and "they were not as beautiful as they are painted, although to some extent they have a human appearance in the face. . . ." These explorers returned home with tales of mermaids, so the myth of the mermaid lingered for decades. I'm not sure about the face of a mermaid, but the manatee bumping up against me has the look of an eggplant with chin and whiskers. Leonard

Early naturalists believed that manatees were unusual tropical walruses. In this illustration from around 1800, the walrus (center) and the bullet-shaped manatee (lower left) *are listed as members of the same family. Today, scientists know that manatees and their relatives, the dugongs, are in the order of animals called Sirenia and are not related to seals and walruses. Sirenians evolved from four-footed land mammals more than sixty million years ago. The closest modern relatives of the Sirenia are elephants and aardvarks. The term* sirenia *comes from the word "sirens," or mermaids, who, according to ancient tales, lured ships to crash against the rocks in the sea. (Courtesy of John E. Reynolds)*

MANATEE FACTS
MANATEE SPECIES

Manatees belong to the order of mammals called sirenians. Today, four species of sirenians exist: one dugong and three manatees. A fifth species, the Steller's sea cow, became extinct in 1768. The manatees include the West African manatee, the Amazonian manatee, and the West Indian manatee. The manatee found in Florida is the West Indian manatee. It is the largest of all living sirenians, about ten feet in length, and weighs more than a ton, or about two thousand pounds. Florida manatees are found in shallow, slow-moving rivers, coastal bays, and estuaries. They prefer waters that are about three to seven feet deep. This habitat provides manatees with sheltered waters for feeding, resting, and rearing their young.

The dugong lives along southwest Pacific coastlines, the Indian coast, and the East African coast. The West African manatee lives in the West African coastal areas from Senegal to Angola. The Amazonian manatee lives in the rivers and lakes along the Amazon River basin.

Dugong, 8–13 feet (2–4 meters)

Steller's Sea Cow, 24–30 feet (7–9 meters)

West African Manatee, 10–13 feet (3–4 meters)

Amazonian Manatee, 10 feet (3 meters)

West Indian Manatee, 10–13 feet (3–4 meters)

15

Dr. Mark Lowe (left) and I check on the captive manatees at Homosassa Springs Wildlife State Park. Mark believes "the next fifteen years will be crucial" in saving the manatee from extinction.

(Top right) *A visitor at Homosassa Springs gets a closeup view of manatees feeding on heads of lettuce. Manatees prefer romaine lettuce.*

Nimoy (Mr. Spock of *Star Trek* fame) once called the manatee a "bewhiskered blimp of an animal."

Beside me is Dr. Mark Lowe, a veterinarian who has been doing weekly checkups on the manatees at Homosassa Springs since 1989. I'm here to help. Homosassa Springs is located about an hour north of Tampa, on Florida's west coast. The manatees here are captive animals. They are big and tame, like huge underwater puppies begging for doggy treats.

"We feed them protein pellets during the checkups," says Mark. "It's basically elephant food. When they come to feed, it allows us to look for sores or other problems that might show up."

I hold out one of the elephant biscuits. A manatee the size of Manhattan pokes his face out of the water. Black beady eyes squint in the bright light. A heavily whiskered snout closes in on the treat. Enormous upper lips flare out and engulf the

I feed a vitamin biscuit to one of the captive manatees. Biologists believe the bristles on a manatee's face are unique in that they can move and help to hold food.

(Top) *Manatees grasp and tear vegetation with their lips and then pass the food back to their grinding teeth.*

Scientists have learned that manatees can renew about 90 percent of the air in their lungs with a single breath. Humans renew about 10 percent in a single breath.

cookie. The manatee's lips astonish me. They seem so flexible. These large, split upper lips work independently of each other almost as if they are face-hands. The stiff, pale bristles covering the lips help draw plants into the manatee's mouth. Scientists also believe that these face bristles are very sensitive. Manatees use these bristles to manipulate objects and explore their world. Bristles help the manatee avoid obstacles, find food, and feel other manatees. It's like having a face full of fingers.

I touch the manatee's head and back. Here the skin is thick, rough, and bumpy, like a dry sponge. Algae and other plants grow along the full length of the manatee. Dr. Lowe tells me the plants growing on manatees' backs don't bother them. I feel the manatee's side and belly. Here the skin is smoother, gray, worn, and as leathery as an old shoe. Like all mammals, manatees grow hair on their bodies. Tough individual hairs, some two inches long, poke out here and there along the sides of the manatee's body. Scientists believe they may act like the lateral lines in fish, sensing motion in the water.

"Manatees have many wonderful adaptations that help them survive in an aquatic world," says Mark. "The skin is continually sloughing off, or shedding, to reduce the buildup of algae."

I look into the manatee's open mouth as it pleads for another biscuit. The mouth is specially designed to eat plants. I see rows of cream-colored molars. Manatees have unique teeth. Front teeth are worn down by the constant grinding of plants and sandy roots. The emerging teeth in the back move up, pushing the whole row of teeth forward. The front ones are pushed out and replaced by newer molars. Amazingly, manatees make new teeth their entire lives. That's why you never see manatee dentists.

Another manatee beside me pokes its snout out of the water. I watch it breathe. Two flaps, or valves, on the manatee's nose open up. These flaps covering the nostrils are as round and large as nickels. The manatee sucks in air, then the flaps close over the nostrils. As soon as the manatee has gulped some air, it submerges. On average, manatees surface to breathe every three to five minutes. If they are very active, manatees may come up for air every thirty seconds. The manatee's heartbeat slows when it submerges, decreasing from up to sixty beats per minute to around thirty. In this resting state, a manatee may stay submerged for up to twenty minutes, sleeping on the river bottom or just below the surface of the water.

We stand and watch the manatees move. I see how they propel through the water by moving their fluke up and down. Manatees steer with their flippers and fluke. Mark and I take hold of the edge of a manatee fluke. The power is awesome. When the manatee wants to go, it goes. Normally manatees swim between three to five miles per hour but can move faster if they need to. They can swim up to twenty miles per hour in short bursts. Mark tells me the fluke is powerful enough to lift an adult human out of the water.

An enormous manatee bumps up against my knee.

"Good morning, Amanda," says Mark. Members of the staff at Homosassa Springs have given names to the eight captive manatees in the park.

Mark points to a deep gash along Amanda's back. "A boat collided with this manatee in 1973," says Mark. "The propellers left a deep wound. We rescued this animal and brought her here for rehabilitation."

I look at Amanda's scar and think about the times I have been in a speeding boat. I think about the hundreds of thousands of powerboats that zip and zoom along Florida's waterways. And

Similar to the tail of a whale or dolphin, a manatee's flat, paddle-shaped tail moves in an up-and-down motion, propelling the animal through the water.

A manatee's slow-moving, passive behavior makes it vulnerable to boat collisions when it surfaces to breathe. The manatee at the bottom of the photo is Amanda.

Throwing fishing line in the waters of Florida is against the law. A manatee can get entangled in fishing line or crab-trap line. Mutilated flippers or even drowning sometimes results.

then I think about the question: Could there be a way to prevent or limit collisions between boats and manatees? Mark tells me collisions with boats are one of the leading causes of manatee deaths in Florida. Posted speed-zone signs are located throughout Florida waters to alert boaters about safe operating speeds when manatees are present.

NATURE DICTIONARY

Algal bloom: *a population explosion of microscopic marine organisms, commonly known as red tide.*

Aquifer: *an underground bed or layer of rock, sand, or gravel containing water*

Blubber: *the fat layer in marine mammals*

Buoyancy: *the ability to float*

Carcass: *the dead body of an animal*

Cold stress: *condition caused by prolonged cold weather that can lead to heat loss and death*

Endangered: *wildlife species whose survival is in jeopardy and in danger of extinction*

Endangered Species Act: *a law, passed by the federal government in 1973, which makes it illegal to "harass, harm, pursue, hunt, shoot, wound, kill, capture, or collect endangered species"*

Extinct: *a plant or animal that no longer exists*

Flatulence: *expelled gases generated in the intestines*

Fluke: *tail*

Herbivore: *an animal that eats mainly plants*

Mammary: *the breast of a female mammal that nourishes young with milk*

Necropsy: *the examination of a dead animal*

Rehabilitation: *restoring an animal to health*

Sediment: *material that settles to the bottom of a river, sea, lake, or other body of water*

Unusually cold weather in Florida can threaten the survival of manatees. At water temperatures below about sixty degrees Fahrenheit, manatees may become sluggish, and they may stop eating. Another threat to manatees is red tide. It can occur when the conditions are right. A harmful algal bloom is a population explosion of tiny marine plants. When these marine creatures build to such huge numbers, a toxin is released that harms manatees. An outbreak of red tide in 1996 caused 150 manatee deaths. The biggest cause of manatee death by humans is collision with boats. Manatees move slowly as they feed in shallow waters. Every few minutes they need to rise to the surface to breathe. As manatees are often found in waters three to seven feet deep, they may not have the depth to dive and escape a fast-moving boat. A boat hull or keel can crush bones and vital organs. Propellers can slash bodies and flukes. If a manatee survives a collision with a boat, it may wear the scar for life. Often these distinctive scar patterns are used to identify individual manatees.

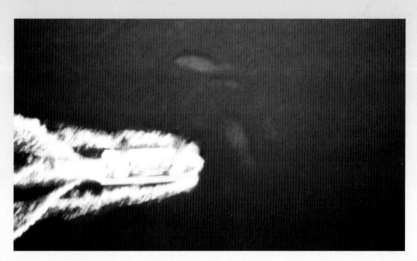

Scientists have studied whether installing propeller guards or boat alarms might reduce the damage or possibility of a collision between boat and manatee. With close to a million registered boats in Florida and only about three thousand manatees left, the problem is huge.

The Crystal River National Wildlife Refuge was established in 1983 for the protection of the endangered West Indian manatee. This refuge preserves the last unspoiled and undeveloped habitat in Kings Bay, Florida, which forms the headwaters of the Crystal River. It's home for approximately 25 percent of Florida's manatee population. Six hundred million gallons of fresh water—at a constant 72 degrees Fahrenheit—flow daily from the natural springs.

(left) *Taking notes on the swimming behavior of a manatee at Tampa's Lowry Park Zoo in Florida*

Chapter Three

MANATEES LOVE FLORIDA

I AM DRIVING NORTH OUT OF TAMPA ON HIGHWAY 19 along the west coast of Florida. As the miles pile up, it doesn't take long to realize I'm in manatee country. If manatees could read, these places would be on every manatee's lips: Weeki Wachee Springs, Homosassa Springs, Crystal River, Rainbow Springs. If you were a manatee, wouldn't you want to spend the winter at a place called Crystal River?

For manatees, it's all about keeping warm in winter. Florida is at the northern end of the West Indian manatee's range. The water is too cold for manatees to survive year-round any farther north. In summer, manatees swim Florida's warm rivers and coastal waters. They may even wander to the waters of Gulf Coast states such as Louisiana, Mississippi, and Texas. On the Atlantic coast they may swim as far as Virginia and the

Carolinas. In winter, manatees seek warm water with temperatures of 70 degrees Fahrenheit or above, and that means hanging out in Florida.

Historically, manatees migrated to the thirty or so warm-water sites around Florida in the winter, November through March. These sites include natural springs and warm-water bays and rivers. Crystal River and Homosassa Springs on the west coast and Blue Spring on the east coast are important sites for large numbers of manatees to spend the winter. For the past two decades or so, manatees have gathered at warm-water discharge areas located near power plants. During the production

Idle speed is the minimum speed that will maintain steerage of a boat. When boating in waters with manatees, always keep eyes peeled for a snout, back, tail, or flipper breaking the surface of the water, or a swirl or flat spot on the water caused by the motion of the manatee's tail when it dives.

During the cold months, tourists gather at Tampa Electric's manatee viewing center.

of electricity, large power turbines are cooled by water. This heated, clean water is released, and manatees love the artificial warm bath.

Manatees have an uncanny ability to find warm water in the winter. The knowledge of Florida's warm-water sites seems to be passed down from generation to generation. Calves learn from their mothers where the springs and power plants are.

Biologists worry about the future of Florida's warm water. The flow of water in certain warm-water springs in the state has dropped sharply. Scientists wonder if development and other human use are affecting much of Florida's groundwater. Florida has one of the fastest-growing populations in the country. Are too many people shrinking the state's natural aquifer, or underground water supply? Another concern is the closing of power plants. If an energy plant shuts down and no longer discharges warm water, what happens to hundreds of manatees that seek out this warm-water refuge in cold weather? The concern over the future of warm water for manatee use has reached the point where scientists, government officials, and others have formed the Warm Water Task Force. This group hopes to develop some long-range ideas about preserving warm-water refuges for future generations of manatees.

The sign up ahead reads Manatee Springs State Park. I can't resist, so I pull the car off the highway and drive down to the entrance. As I park, Florida's afternoon thunderclouds darken the sky overhead. I grab my raincoat and make for the boardwalk. I haven't walked ten feet when the clouds spill their contents. The rain comes down in bathtubs. I remember reading somewhere that every day over 150 billion gallons of rainwater fall in Florida. It seems as if a billion gallons are falling on me right now.

All this water has to go somewhere. I watch the water seep into the ground. I know that stretching beneath north Florida is a huge bed of underground limestone. The runoff percolates down, dissolving the soft rock into "Swiss cheese." The ground under north Florida looks like a sponge.

This rain is good for manatees, whether they know it or not. The rain replenishes the huge volumes of water in the natural springs. As hundreds of manatees migrate from cold coastal waters to the warm-water springs each winter, the springs are lifesavers. I look into the rain-hammered surface of the spring. There's not a manatee in sight. The Spanish moss hangs like gray, wet beards. I'm soaked to the bone. Time to make like a manatee and swim away.

More than 100 million gallons of fresh water gush every day from Manatee Springs, located at Manatee Springs State Park, six miles west of Chiefland, Florida.

Walking back to the car, I realized how precious warm water is to manatees. I remember learning a few days earlier in Tampa that manatees can die of "cold stress." I visited a low, windowless beige building, the home of Florida's Fish and Wildlife's Marine Mammal Pathology Laboratory. (*Pathology* is the study of disease and causes of death.)

If a manatee dies in Florida and it can be retrieved, there's a good chance that biologists Andy Garrett and Alex Costidis will see it.

Before the 1970s, no one dissected manatees. In 1973, the manatee became one of the first animals to be federally protected under the Endangered Species Act. In 1974, scientists started to perform necropsies (the examinations of dead animals) on manatees to learn why they were dying. In more than thirty years of studying manatee carcasses, biologists have learned a great deal about manatee biology and threats to the animal's survival.

"Sometimes a collision with a boat doesn't always leave ghastly cuts on a manatee's body," says Andy. "The hull of a boat can bang against a manatee, leaving no visible marks outside, and yet inside, there are broken ribs and damaged organs."

"Manatees have dense and heavy skin," says Alex. "As a matter of fact, it looks very much like elephant skin. Elephants are the closest land relative of the manatee. Elephants and manatees have many features in common: thick skin, tooth replacement, flexible lips, nails on their flippers."

The biologists tell me a manatee has a digestive system like a horse. They have huge intestines that help break down plant material. A manatee's large intestine can measure almost as long as seventy feet and weigh as much as 250 pounds. In comparison, most humans have large intestines fewer than three feet in length. Dr. John Reynolds, one of Florida's leading manatee experts, says that not only is a lot of heat generated inside those extraordinarily long intestines but also an amazing

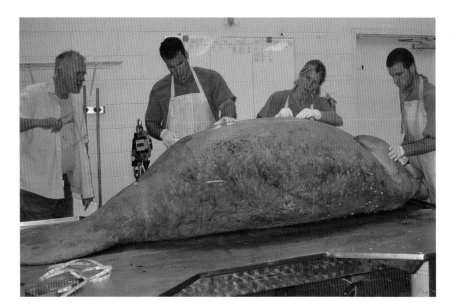

(top) *As I look on, biologists begin the necropsy of a manatee. By examining the manatee carcass, scientists can learn important information, such as the weight of the animal, its age, and perhaps why the animal died.*
(bottom) *Zookeepers at Lowry Park Zoo care for an abandoned manatee named Buttonwood.*

amount of flatulence, or gas. Reynolds and colleague Butch Rommel surmise that all this gas may even contribute to helping the manatee control its buoyancy in the water.

Andy and Alex show me the skull of a manatee. "In many species of animal, we learn their age by making a horizontal cut on one of their teeth and reading the annual growth rings," says Alex. "It's like reading the growth rings on a tree stump. Each individual ring represents a year of life." Alex explains that determining the age of manatees is not so easy. While dolphins keep their teeth for life, manatees constantly replace their teeth. Instead of using manatee teeth to learn the animal's age, biologists use manatee ear bones. "We discover the age of the manatee by counting the annual rings in its ear bone," says Alex.

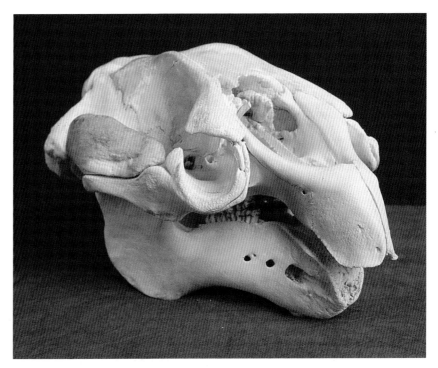

Biologists from Tampa's Lowry Park Zoo prepare to release a rehabilitated manatee back into the wild.

The skull of a manatee. Manatees have been swimming in Florida's waters for more than a million years.

Andy explains that because there are so many perils in the wild, many manatees die between the ages of zero and ten years. He says this is nowhere near the life expectancy of sixty years. Alex tells me that their lab and other rehabilitation facilities in Florida have conducted more than four thousand necropsies on manatee carcasses. Although one of those animals had been as old as fifty-nine years, the average age of the manatees recovered was seven. The lab has discovered that about 30 percent of all manatee deaths are caused by watercraft collisions. If a manatee gets bumped by a boat or trapped in cold water and is not seriously wounded or hurt, there's a chance of rehabilitation. There are three federally permitted manatee rescue and rehabilitation facilities in Florida: Tampa's Lowry Park Zoo, Miami Seaquarium, and SeaWorld Orlando. The goal of these centers is to rescue hurt manatees, rehabilitate them, and release them back into the wild.

 **MANATEE FACTS**
THE REAL NATIVE OF FLORIDA

Ever since human beings could throw a stone or hurl a spear, they've hunted animals for meat. Woolly mammoths, whales, bison, elephants, among others, have all been on the menu for man. Some animals, such as Steller's sea cow, the dodo bird, and the passenger pigeon, have even been hunted to extinction. For perhaps ten thousand years, early inhabitants of Florida killed and hunted manatees for food.

Some people wonder if manatees are native to Florida. They also wonder how long they've lived in the state. Bones of Florida manatees have been found in the state's sediment dating back more than a million years. Human beings arrived in Florida many thousands of years after the manatees. So maybe the real question is, Who is the native resident of Florida—human or manatee?

Alex (center) points out the "migrating teeth" in a manatee skull to me (left) and Andy (right) at Florida's Fish and Wildlife's Marine Mammal Pathology Lab.

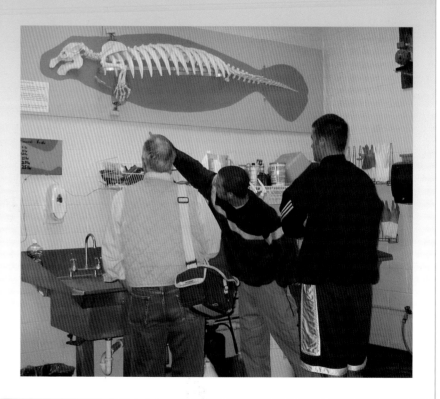

A zookeeper at Tampa's Lowry Park Zoo hand-feeds a forty-eight-pound newborn male manatee called Buttonwood. This abandoned baby manatee was malnourished and dehydrated when found. It was recovered in Buttonwood Bay, near Marco Island. Manatees are nicknamed after the area from where they are recovered. Buttonwood slurps infant-baby formula loaded with vitamin supplements.

For the first time, I come face-to-face with a manatee while snorkeling at Crystal River, Florida.

(left) *Manatees have dark, marble-sized eyes. Though small, a manatee's eyes can see objects distinctly and can see different colors, too. A thin, transparent eyelid can slide across each eye for protection.*

Chapter Four

MANATEES UP CLOSE AND PERSONAL

I JAM MY FACE MASK TIGHT AGAINST MY SKIN, bite down hard on the mouthpiece of the snorkel, and slip underwater. Welcome to the marvelously muffled, fantastically illuminated, deliciously slow-motion underwater world of the manatee. Here's where, I think, I will come as close as I can to knowing this marine creature—side by side, in its own watery habitat.

I'm snorkeling with a dozen fourth-graders in the clean, shallow water of Crystal River, Florida, on a cool morning in

(top) *A volunteer warden at Crystal River National Wildlife Refuge paddles his kayak during his watch, keeping a close eye on both snorklers and manatees.*

Scientists have calculated that manatees spend about six to eight hours a day feeding and two to twelve hours a day resting. Resting manatees may stay submerged for up to twenty minutes.

February. Before we even touch the water with a flipper, our whole group has a lesson in manatee etiquette. The captain of the snorkeling and dive boat explains a few rules: let the manatees come to you, don't chase or harass the animals, don't surround them, don't disturb nursing calves, and don't feed manatees. Our small pod of wet-suited snorklers fans out, minding our manatee manners.

At the major warm-water springs in Crystal River National Wildlife Refuge, protected areas are set aside for manatees. These areas are safe places for manatees to retreat, to nurse, and to feed. Sometimes these places are cordoned off with ropes, flags, or signs to prevent boaters and swimmers from approaching too close.

I am snorkeling with two students, Kalli and John. We move to within a few feet of a roped-off area. A manatee warden in a kayak paddles by. Through the four-inch window of my snorkel mask, I squint to see six manatees stacked up like cord wood, sleeping on the bottom. Big gray logs. I point as a young manatee rises to the surface and swims in our direction.

The four-foot-long manatee comes close. We look into its eyes, little black marbles. Kalli and John snap away with their yellow underwater cameras. We watch the manatee swim off in undulating motions powered by its broad, flat tail.

We bob to the surface and hear some students calling excitedly beside the boat. We swim closer to take a look.

"Quick! A manatee's eating the line!" calls one student.

We look underwater to see a manatee "mouthing" the boat's anchor line.

"It looks as if he's using dental floss to clean his teeth," says Kalli. Manatees love mouthing things: other manatees, logs, anchor rope. Scientists believe manatees can learn by tasting objects. For instance, male manatees may locate females ready

Manatees are curious animals and sometimes investigate their world by mouthing objects, such as this boat line.

(top) *Fourth-graders from Mrs. Crowe's class observe a manatee in the wild.*

(bottom) *Manatees often rest in shallow areas. Scientists believe that when manatees rise to the surface to breathe, boats sometimes strike them. That's because they can't dive quickly or deeply enough to avoid getting hit.*

to breed by following chemical cues and tasting the water.

I peel away from the group to explore on my own. I haven't gone very far when a young manatee swims into my view. The manatee seems curious and comes alongside. We swim together. I reach out and scratch its flank, and the manatee does the most amazing thing. It emits four or five "clicks," almost like soft chirping. And then the manatee rolls, as if to say, "Now this side, please." I scratch its other side, and again I hear the underwater clicking noises. It rolls. We repeat this human-manatee interaction: scratching, rolling, and clicking two or three more times. The whole episode lasts less than a minute, but it feels longer. Finally, the young manatee veers away. Manatee experts tell me that besides touching and seeing,

When it was time for Elizabeth Crowe's fourth-grade class from Panama City Beach, Florida, to study an endangered species, the class chose the manatee. The students were required to research the manatee's habitat as well as to find the answers to some tough questions: How has the environment of the manatee changed over time? What changes have led to its present status? The highlight of the entire project came when Mrs. Crowe's students got in the water and swam with the manatees. The class is pictured above with me, left, and Mrs. Crowe, right, at the Lowry Park Zoo, Tampa, Florida.

mother and calf communicate by vocalizing. With a constant chatter of clicks, squeaks, and squeals, mother and calf stay in contact, even in very murky water.

I pop to the surface and blink. "Wow, did that really happen?" I say to myself. I just had this awesome and private encounter with a wild manatee. I feel like shouting out to the group that they, too, should come and try this. But, of course, I don't. I believe these brief, exhilarating encounters with wild animals are gifts. We should accept them as private reminders that the creatures we share this planet with are unique and mysterious and beautiful.

My excitement is tinged with guilt, though. I know I shouldn't touch a manatee. I believe in the "no touch" policy when it comes to wild animals. Wild animals remain wild when man does not interfere with their behavior. The naturalist part of me says, "Don't touch," but to satisfy my human curiosity, I reach out. While I struggle with this dilemma on a personal scale, Floridians are grappling with just how close humans and manatees should get.

Some groups in Florida believe people should not be allowed to "swim with the manatees" or touch them. And there are others, such as diving and snorkeling companies, that believe it's okay to snorkel with wild manatees and okay to touch them.

I raise the issue with the fourth-graders after our snorkeling trip with the manatees in Crystal River. Should people be allowed to swim with manatees? Why or why not? Many of the students loved snorkeling with manatees. I hear reactions such as "Way cool!", "Awesome!", "The most amazing trip of my life." But after some reflection, Kalli speaks up and says, "Even though it was fun for us, I don't think people should be allowed to swim with manatees or touch them because it disturbs their peacefulness."

It's the old idea of what one does is fine, but if the thousands of people that search for manatees each year wanted to touch, rather than simply look at manatees, the pressure on the animals would be too much. "Look, but don't touch" may be the best way to mind your manatee manners. And besides, people actually have the most to gain by remaining at a distance when they spot a manatee in the water. By quietly observing manatees, snorkelers will get a rare opportunity to see the natural behavior of these unique animals.

The one thing swimming with the wild manatees did for all of us was make us advocates for manatees. But in the end, I agree with Kalli. Who knows? Maybe some day people visiting Florida's warm-water springs and rivers may talk about the

A manatee enjoys some lettuce.

MANATEE FACTS
SWIMMING WITH MANATEES

Save the Manatee Club was established in 1981 by former Florida Governor Bob Graham and singer-songwriter Jimmy Buffett. The club was begun so the public could participate in conservation efforts to save endangered manatees from extinction.

While Save the Manatee Club is not opposed to people being in the water when manatees are present, it has established the following guidelines for sharing the water with manatees:

- *No touching*

- *No riding*

- *No poking*

- *No feeding or giving them water*

- *No chasing*

- *No surrounding or any actions that might separate a mother and a calf*

(right) *Newborn manatee calves can swim to the surface on their own. They can also vocalize with their mother soon after birth.*

good old days when people could snorkel with the manatees. Can you imagine that? They actually got in the water and touched a manatee. Those were the days.

Some swimmers don't understand how touching a manatee can be harmful to the animal. Save the Manatee Club believes touching manatees can alter their behavior in the wild, perhaps causing them to leave warm-water areas and making them susceptible to potential harm. When manatees are in colder water, they expend valuable energy just to keep warm. This leaves little energy left for other important body functions, such as digestion. Pursuing a manatee while diving, swimming, or boating may inadvertently separate a mother and her calf.

Manatee calves are dependent on their mothers for up to

two years. Mothers not only feed their calves, but they also teach them all the things they need to know to survive on their own. Calves who are separated from their mothers may get lost. For example, if a mother swims away while a calf is being petted, the calf may not find his way back to her and could ultimately die without her. In recent years, dependent calf mortality has increased considerably. This may be due, in part, to mother and calf separation.

People get very emotional about manatees. If you want to drive your boat fast and you have to slow down because manatees are nearby, you get angry. If you want to build a house along a waterway but can't because manatees are in the area and they are protected, you get angry. How can people get fighting mad about such a gentle, harmless creature as a manatee? Yet, they do. There are many people who love manatees and want to protect them. And there are those who think manatees are

MANATEE FACTS
IT'S THE LAW!

Consider the following:

1. *Manatees are federally protected under the Endangered Species Act of 1973 and the Marine Mammal Protection Act of 1972.*
2. *The Florida Manatee Sanctuary Act of 1978 also protects them in Florida.*
3. *Florida manatees are one of the most endangered marine mammals living in coastal waters of the United States today.*
4. *Florida is one of the fastest-developing states in America. Every day, about one thousand new people move to Florida. With so many rivers and coasts to explore in Florida, there are close to one million people who love to go boating.*

Scientists have found that juvenile manatees can be completely on their own by the time they are two years old.

Manatee calves grow quickly. From a 3-foot, 66-pound baby, a manatee can grow to an 8-foot, 550-pound youngster in two years.

While many people express their support for saving the manatee—Florida's gentle giant—it will take a huge commitment by Florida's citizens.

overrated nuisances, nothing more than big gray blobs, or even "speed bumps." They say the only positive thing about manatees is they're good eating.

Wow! One side wants to hug them; the other wants to eat them. How do you bring such opposing sides together? The people and lawmakers of Florida face a huge challenge. Can Florida find a way to bring manatee lovers and manatee haters together? Can Florida make room for an endangered species like a manatee along with a growing population of people who love water and boats? Will future generations of Florida school kids experience one of their state's most amazing mammals living in the wild?

Or will Florida allow the manatee to go extinct? One hundred years from now, will manatees be found only in books, on computer screens, and as stuffed specimens in nature museums? Might people one day ask, Why didn't we save the manatee?

Biologists prepare to release a manatee into the wild.

FURTHER READING

John E. Reynolds III is one of Florida's leading manatee experts and has written two great books for older readers: *Mysterious Manatees* (University Press of Florida, 2003) and *Dolphins, Whales, and Manatees of Florida: A Guide to Sharing Their World* (University Press of Florida, 2003). Younger readers might want to read *Manatees* by Kathy Feeney (Northword Press, 2001) and *The Manatee* by Alvin, Virginia, and Robert Silverstein and Laura Silverstein Nunn (Millbrook Press, 1995).

WEB SITES
(These sites were active at time of publication.)

You can learn more about manatees as well adopt a manatee by visiting the Save the Manatee Club's Web site at www.savethemanatee.org

Other good Web sites about manatees include:

www.floridaconservation.org/psm

www.lowryparkzoo.com

www.miamiseaquarium.com

www.seaworld.org

www.sirenian.org

You can also learn more about manatees and other animals on Steve Swinburne's Web site at www.steveswinburne.com

Drawing of a manatee by Joe Bauer Griffin, age ten, Florida

INDEX

Blue Spring State Park, 10
Columbus, Christopher, 14
Crystal River, 23, 24, 31, 35
Crystal River National Wildlife Refuge, 32
dugong, 11, 14, 15
Endangered Species Act, 7, 20, 26, 37
Florida Fish and Wildlife Marine Mammal
    Pathology Laboratory, 26, 28
Homosassa Springs Wildlife State Park, 13, 16, 19, 23, 24
Lowry Park Zoo, 23, 26, 27, 28, 29, 34
Manatees
    Amazonian manatee, 15
    breathing, 18, 19, 21
    breeding, 8
    calves, 8, 24, 35, 36, 37
    diet, 7, 11, 16
    flippers, 19, 20
    fluke, 19, 20
    heartbeat, 19
    intestines, 26–27
    lips, 18
    range, 8, 9
    skin, 14, 18, 26
    skull, 27
    speed, 19
    teeth, 18, 28
    West African manatee, 15
    West Indian manatee, 15
Manatee Springs State Park, 25
mermaids, 14
necropsy, 20, 26, 28
powerboats, 19, 20, 21, 26, 28
power plants, 24
red tide, 7, 20, 21
Save the Manatee Club, 36, 39
Steller's sea cow, 11, 15